Your Body for Life

Emotions

From birth to old age

Richard Spilsbury

Raintree is an imprint of Capstone Global Library Limited, a company incorporated in England and Wales having its registered office at 7 Pilgrim Street, London, EC4V 6LB – Registered company number: 6695582

To contact Raintree please phone 0845 6044371, fax + 44 (0) 1865 312263, or email myorders@raintreepublishers.co.uk. Customers from outside the UK please telephone +44 1865 312262.

Edited by Andrew Farrow, Adam Miller, and Adrian Vigliano
Designed by Cynthia Della-Rovere
Original illustrations © Capstone Global Library Ltd
Illustrated by HL Studios Ltd
Picture research by Mica Brancic
Production by Victoria Fitzgerald
Originated by Capstone Global Library Ltd
Printed and bound in China by Leo Paper Products Ltd

ISBN 978 1 406 25022 0 (hardback)
16 15 14 13 12
10 9 8 7 6 5 4 3 2 1

ISBN 978 1 406 25029 9 (paperback)
17 16 15 14 13
10 9 8 7 6 5 4 3 2 1

British Library Cataloguing in Publication Data
Spilsbury, Richard
Emotions. – (Your body for life)
152.4-dc23
A full catalogue record for this book is available from the British Library.

Acknowledgements

We would like to thank the following for permission to reproduce photographs: Alamy pp. 10 (© Anne-Marie Palmer), 16 (© Asiaselects), 18 (© Bob Ebbesen), 23 (© Lou Linwei), 27 (© Dan Atkin), 30 (© Richard Newton), 32 (© PhotoAlto sas), 34 (© Andrew Fox), 37 (© Denkou Images), 40 (© Brian Finestone), 44 (© Robert Preston Photography), 46 (© Ingram Publishing), 52 (© Marmaduke St. John); Corbis pp. 33 (Reuters/Rodrigo Arias), 41 (cultura/© Nancy Honey), 42 (Blend Images/© Hill Street Studios), 45 (© Gary Salter), 51 (Reuters/© Helen Atkinson), 54 (© Ronnie Kaufman), 55 (© Creasource); Getty Images pp. 13 (Reza), 21 (Thinkstock Images/Comstock Images), 29 (Majid Saeedi), 38 (Photographer's Choice/Peter Dazeley); Science Photo Library p. 9 (Wellcome Dept. Of Imageing Neuroscience); Shutterstock pp. 4 (© Sergei Bachlakov), 7 (© Jakub Cejpek), 15 (© StockLite), 22 (© Rob Hainer), 24 (© Dmitriy Shironosov), 31 (© Sydneymills), 42 (© Vicente Barcelo Varona), 49 (© Monkey Business Images).

Cover photograph of a timid girl hiding behind a boy reproduced with permission of Corbis (© Lucidio Studio Inc).

Cover photograph of happy adult woman reproduced with permission of Shutterstock (© Diego Cervo).

Cover photograph of upset boy against a wall reproduced with permission of Shutterstock (© Mikael Damkier).

Cover photograph of handsome young man reproduced with permission of Shutterstock (© Antonio Jorge Nunes).

We would like to thank Ann Fullick for her invaluable help in the preparation of this book.

Every effort has been made to contact copyright holders of any material reproduced in this book. Any omissions will be rectified in subsequent printings if notice is given to the publisher.

Disclaimer

Contents

The world of emotions 4

Infancy: birth to three years old 14

Childhood: four to ten years old 22

Adolescence: ten to eighteen years old 30

Adulthood 42

Old age 48

Quiz 56

Facts and figures 58

Glossary 60

Find out more 62

Index 64

Some words are printed in **bold**, like this. You can find out what they mean by looking in the glossary on pages 60–61.

The world of emotions

Joy at seeing a live concert and anger at being treated unfairly are powerful feelings. These are just two of a whole range of emotions that we all feel throughout our lives. The ways we experience emotions vary enormously, from blushing with embarrassment to shaking with anger. We express our emotions in different ways, too, ranging from words to non-verbal communication such as frowning or making a gesture like a "thumbs up".

Emotions for all

The emotion one person feels may be shared by many other people responding to the same event. At a sporting event, when the home team scores, thousands of the team's fans feel great happiness and excitement – while the rest of the crowd feels despair!

Emotion or mood?

The words emotion and mood are often used interchangeably, but scientists say they are different things. Here are some of the very general differences, but note that this is a simplification, and moods and emotions are linked. For example, the emotion of short-term grief may turn into a long-term low mood or **depression**:

	Emotions	**Moods**
Cause	A specific event	Often general and unclear
Length	Very brief (seconds or minutes)	Longer than emotions (hours or days)
Type	Distinct (for example, sadness)	General (for example, negative)
Signs	Distinct facial expressions	No distinct expressions

Emotional society

Emotions are incredibly important for human social behaviour. They affect the way we understand and react to the world around us and to our friends, families, and other groups. **Empathy** is the way we imagine how others might feel, based on our own understanding of emotions. For example, we may comfort a friend who is sad because we know how sadness feels and want to make our friend feel better. The promise of feeling emotions in the future can also motivate us to take action. For example, we get all our homework done so that we can feel the pleasure of a free weekend.

Personal experience

Everyone feels emotions slightly differently. That is partly because our personal experience of emotions depends on what has happened to us in the past. For example, someone who felt very scared by one horror film might feel nervous about seeing another one, because of memories of that strong emotion. Emotions may also include what we think we should feel. Some people cry at funerals because they feel personal loss – but also because it is the expected emotional response to death. The range and strength of emotions we feel never stop changing throughout our lives, partly because our experiences and understanding of other people and their emotions change, too.

Enormous range of emotions

How many emotions do people feel? A scientist called Robert Plutchik created a simplified chart summarizing a wide range of emotions. He decided on eight major, or primary, emotions, with each having lots of variations from weak to strong, for example, feeling annoyed is a weaker version of rage. These emotions combine to create human feelings, for example, ecstasy and admiration combine to create love. He also showed emotions that were mixtures of the primary emotions. For example, disappointment combines surprise and sadness. Can you think of any emotions that seem to be missing from this chart?

Plutchik's wheel of emotions

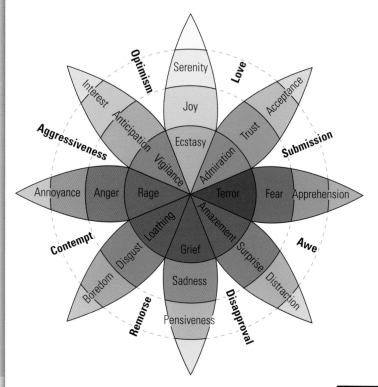

Triggering emotions

Our emotions can be triggered, or set off, in lots of different ways. Some triggers are obvious, like when we feel sadness when someone close to us is injured or upset. Some emotions are triggered by sounds, such as people's fear when they hear a dentist's drill or calmness when they hear the sea. Tastes and smells are triggers, too. The smell of the chlorine used to purify swimming pools makes some people happy, because it reminds them of fun times in the water. Some triggers are more subtly built into our nervous responses, and it is not always obvious why they happen. For example, some people feel agitated when they enter a red room, but they feel calm in a blue room.

Triggers work because our brains remember experiences that set off strong emotions before. Some people continue experiencing strong emotions in reaction to a situation even if they are repeatedly triggered. For example, actors in long-running plays may still experience a great thrill each time they walk out on stage, because they have enjoyed it in the past. But sometimes the repeated experience of a trigger can dull responses. For example, people who play a lot of violent video games may not feel as much revulsion to the real violence they see on the news as they did before they started to play those games.

Spot a fake smile

People smile spontaneously when they are happy. With a genuine smile, there is a particular combination of changes to facial muscles and the overlying skin that lasts for a few seconds. Sometimes people put on fake smiles to pretend they are happy, for example, while politely greeting a new co-worker. Most people can spot fake smiles easily because the facial expression is not quite right. Here is how to tell:

	Real	Fake
Mouth		
Curves upwards at edges	●	●
Stretched wide	●	●
Cheeks raised	●	
Eyes wrinkle	●	
Face symmetrical	●	
Longer than 4 seconds		●

Spreading feelings

The emotions we see in others have a big impact on our own. When we look at another person, our eyes spend most of the time scanning the other person's face. This is so we can rapidly spot any subtle changes in facial expression that might indicate what the person is feeling. For example, raised eyebrows suggest a person is feeling surprised or shocked. Being good at spotting emotions can help us react to danger more quickly or be more empathetic to others. Our reactions to the changes we see in other people's emotions can happen fast. For example, excitement, panic, or grief may sweep swiftly through whole crowds, because emotions expressed by one person trigger the person next to him or her, and so on.

Reliving strong emotions

Most people might be scared stiff just at the thought of attempting a stunt like this, but some people overcome those feelings of fear and even look forward to the thrill it will give them.

Phobias

Do you know anyone who is afraid of flying, spiders, or the dentist? This level of **phobia** is described as simple. People with simple phobias might organize their lives specifically to avoid the objects or situations that scare them. Complex phobias cause more extreme reactions. For example, agoraphobia is the fear of open spaces. People with this complex phobia may be so desperate to avoid the emotion that they hardly ever leave their homes.

Emotional centres

We feel emotions in our brain. The human brain is made up of lots of interconnected **neurons** (nerve **cells**) that form different parts, or centres, with differing roles. The centres of emotional activity are in the inner part of the **forebrain**, which is the front part of the brain. Different **brain centres** deal with different emotions. For example, the **hypothalamus** deals with emotions of pleasure and misery, while the **amygdala** is involved with anger, anxiety, and depression. We know this because if doctors **stimulate** these centres artificially in patients during brain surgery, the patients feel the same emotions as if they were responding to a real-life situation.

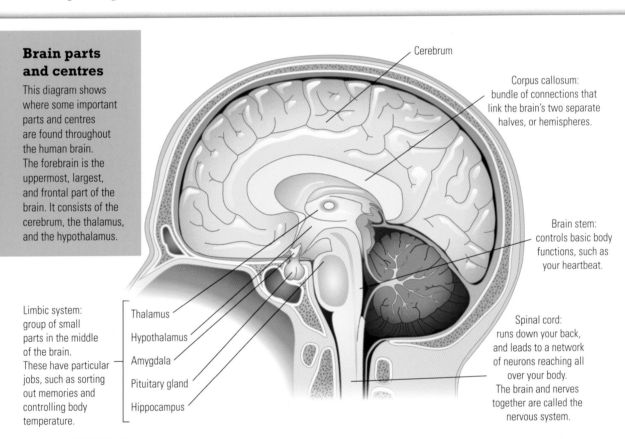

Brain parts and centres

This diagram shows where some important parts and centres are found throughout the human brain. The forebrain is the uppermost, largest, and frontal part of the brain. It consists of the cerebrum, the thalamus, and the hypothalamus.

Limbic system: group of small parts in the middle of the brain. These have particular jobs, such as sorting out memories and controlling body temperature.

Thalamus
Hypothalamus
Amygdala
Pituitary gland
Hippocampus

Cerebrum

Corpus callosum: bundle of connections that link the brain's two separate halves, or hemispheres.

Brain stem: controls basic body functions, such as your heartbeat.

Spinal cord: runs down your back, and leads to a network of neurons reaching all over your body. The brain and nerves together are called the nervous system.

AMAZING BUT TRUE!

Pass it on

The human brain has about 100 billion neurons. Impulses move through each neuron to the next across thousands of tiny junctions called **synapses**. In a synapse, impulses reach the end of one neuron, causing it to produce many **neurotransmitter** molecules. These move across a tiny gap to receptors on the next neuron. The receptors start off the impulse again. This whole process can take just a few thousandths of a second.

AMAZING BUT TRUE!

Brain for smelling

Alligators have the same structures in their forebrain as humans, but in alligators these structures are used primarily to process smells, not emotions! Smell is an essential sense for alligators for finding prey and knowing where other alligators are. Getting enough to eat and being able to either mate or avoid fighting with others are critical skills for survival. Biologists use this evidence from alligators to support the importance of emotions for survival in humans and their societies.

Chemicals of emotion

When people pet their cats or dogs, it makes them feel happy. Sensory receptors in the skin produce electrical nerve impulses that move between several neurons to the brain. Special chemicals called neurotransmitters allow the impulses to move between the neurons. Some neurotransmitters are found only in the brain and allow brain neurons in different centres to communicate with each other. We experience emotions partly because of the levels of neurotransmitters such as **serotonin** in the brain. For example, people feel happier when levels of serotonin are high or in balance between several of their brain centres.

Glands throughout the body produce other chemicals called **hormones**, which play an important part in how we experience emotions. One of the most important glands we have is the pea-sized **pituitary gland**. The hypothalamus controls the levels of hormones made by the pituitary gland, based on information sensed by the brain before and during emotions. Pituitary hormones flow into the blood, where they pass around the body and control how other glands work. For example, pituitary hormones make the **adrenal glands** (near the kidneys) secrete **adrenaline**. This chemical makes us feel excited or angry.

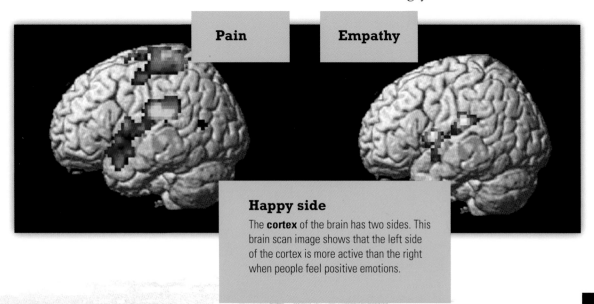

Pain

Empathy

Happy side
The **cortex** of the brain has two sides. This brain scan image shows that the left side of the cortex is more active than the right when people feel positive emotions.

Feeling emotions

Hormones and neurotransmitters cause bodily responses to different emotions. For example, people who are nervous typically start to sweat and get a dry mouth, and those who are feeling calm or content have a slow heartbeat. Some of the same responses may be seen in different emotions, for example, trembling and feeling a heart "racing" both happen when feeling love and when feeling terror.

Scientists divide up the typical responses into two sets: "**fight or flight**" or "rest and digest". Fight-or-flight responses prepare the body to react to danger, while rest-and-digest responses prepare people for situations with no danger, when they can relax and use their energy for digesting food. Both are part of our survival **instincts**. Instincts are types of behaviour that we do not learn – they are just part of the way our brain works. Instincts often affect the way our body works and the way we react to a particular **stimulus**.

Face changes

People around the world almost universally recognize frowns as a sign of sadness or disapproval, and smiles as a sign of friendliness. The wide range of facial expressions of emotions is made possible by slight changes in shape of 43 facial muscles. The movements are controlled by the cerebral cortex.

Fight-or-flight responses

Imagine someone is walking through a park when a tiger suddenly appears from behind a tree. Seeing the tiger would almost certainly cause a sudden and automatic feeling of fear. The range of responses in organs all over the body have particular roles to play in preparing a person to fight or to flee:

Structure	Response	Reason
Heart	Beats faster and more powerfully	More blood to the muscles, to supply glucose and oxygen for energy
Lungs	Breathe faster	More oxygen into the blood
Salivary glands	Dry mouth, as less saliva is produced	No need to digest food
Stomach	Digestion reduced	More blood to the muscles
Liver	Releases more glucose from storage	Energy into the blood
Skin	Gets cold and paler	More blood directed to the heart, lungs, and muscles
Pupils	Dilate (get wider)	Take in more light to see better
Muscles	Tense up and may shake	Ready to run or fight

Showing emotions

People show their emotions to others in many different ways. These include facial expressions such as smiling and grimacing as well as words or sounds, including saying "I love you", or shouting with rage. We use many other types of body language, for example, making a fist when we are angry or putting our head in our hands when we are sad.

A facial expression such as a smile is a standard emotional response for most people, but some people respond in ways that are unexpected or even inappropriate. For example, some people find themselves laughing in situations that most people find upsetting. This is more typical in younger people who have less social experience than adults. It is often because they do not know exactly how to react or are embarrassed to show their real emotions.

AMAZING BUT TRUE!

No disgust

In 2000, doctors studied the emotions of a young man who suffered damage to one part of his forebrain. They discovered that, as a result, he found it much more difficult than healthy volunteers to feel disgust. For example, when asked, "If you were hungry would you eat a bowl of soup that had been stirred with an unwashed fly swatter?" the volunteers consistently answered "no", but the young man repeatedly said "yes"!

Emotional development

The way we feel about ourselves and towards other people depends on many different aspects of our lives. Some of these are physical or biological. For example, people born blind, deaf, or mute may express emotions differently from others. People with certain physical disabilities may be unable to express emotions normally because it is hard for them to control their body or facial muscles. Some people with a disability called autism may find it difficult to recognize facial expressions in others.

The environments we live in also affect emotions in a wide range of ways. For example:

- People who eat healthy diets, get plenty of exercise, and live in clean and spacious surroundings may experience more positive emotions than people who live in the opposite conditions.

- A head injury in a car crash could damage the brain centres responsible for processing emotions.

- Many firefighters who rescued the injured and collected dead bodies after the 11 September 2001 terrorist attacks – when terrorists hijacked aeroplanes and flew them into buildings in New York and Washington, DC in the United States – still cannot sleep or concentrate, overreact to loud noises or alarms, and feel hopeless and guilty about surviving.

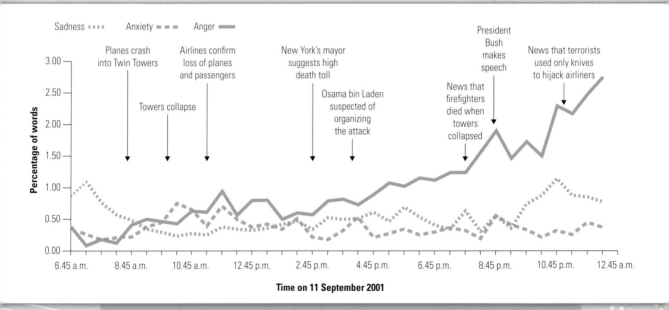

Emotions of 11 September 2001

This graph shows how the emotions expressed in pager messages after the 2001 terrorist attacks changed. Over time, the emotions of sadness and anxiety about the victims were overtaken by anger. This happened as people saw more news reports and developments about the story.

Impact of society

Our emotions are also a result of the people we live with and know. People who grow up in loving, supportive, and stable families may experience fewer negative emotions than people who suffer **neglect** or **abuse** from family members.

Culture also affects emotion. For example, in traditional Japanese culture, it is inappropriate for adults to display anger and is normal to smile in many social situations. A 2010 study found that Japanese people therefore judge the emotions of others based more on the tone of their voice than their facial expression. The opposite is true of Dutch people.

Regardless of culture and the other aspects of their lives, people around the world from very different backgrounds and environments feel and express emotions in similar ways. There is a standard path of emotional development for most of us as we grow older, from birth to old age. This book follows that journey.

Holding hands around the world

In some parts of the world, such as Afghanistan, male friends hold hands without embarrassment. This would be considered very embarrassing for many men in countries such as the United Kingdom, because it might suggest to others that they are homosexual when they are not.

AMAZING BUT TRUE!

Brain training

In 2004, scientists compared brain activity in monks (religious men) who were in training to that of experienced monks who had meditated for over 10,000 hours. Meditating is silently concentrating and focusing on particular thoughts. In the test, both sets of monks meditated about compassion (feeling loving kindness for people). Scientists found that the trained monks had much greater activity in the brain regions responsible for positive, happy emotions than the monks in training. This may be proof that people can train their brain to feel stronger emotions.

Infancy: birth to three years old

At birth, the brain is about a quarter of the size of an adult brain. By the age of three, it will normally have tripled in size, to be near the size of an adult brain. In that short time, the brain develops billions of new neurons and makes connections between parts of the brain, so that it can process information and feel and express many emotions. In this period, a human being also typically transforms from a wholly dependent individual to a very active, noisy, and increasingly independent one. How do emotions change throughout this period?

The first few months

Babies are born able to express four main emotions. These are distress, relaxation, excitement, and surprise. All are accompanied by typical facial expressions, voice sounds (or vocalizations), and changes in behaviour or activity:

- Distress: A distressed baby shows increased movement, which sometimes includes grasping by the arms, an increase in heart rate, a flushed face, and crying. This is usually a response to hunger or discomfort – for example, due to gas or a wet nappy – but it can also be caused by other stimuli, including loud noises or pain caused by infections.

- Relaxation: Relaxed babies close their eyes and their muscles relax. They may also gurgle quietly and examine their hands and feet. Relaxation often follows being comforted, fed, or having a nappy changed.

- Excitement: Excited babies smile, wriggle, and flap their arms and legs, and they sometimes make excited babbling sounds. These signs of excitement appear when they experience familiar, pleasurable events, such as going to the park or seeing a favourite family member or friend, toy, book, or television programme.

- Surprise: Surprised babies' eyes may open wide, they become quieter and still, and their heart rate slows. Babies may be surprised and interested, rather than distressed, by unexpected sounds or unfamiliar objects.

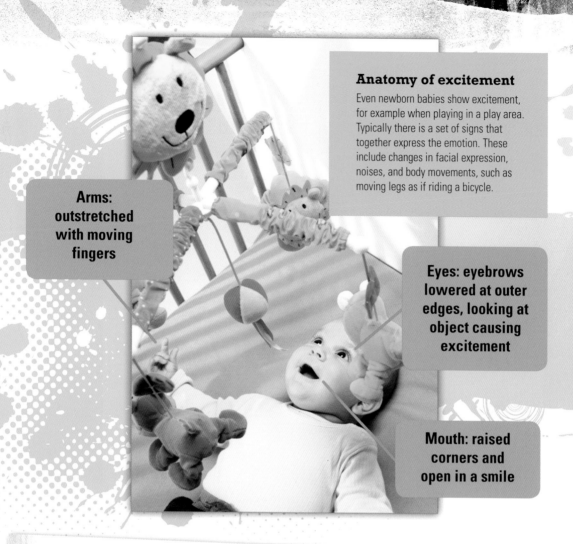

Anatomy of excitement

Even newborn babies show excitement, for example when playing in a play area. Typically there is a set of signs that together express the emotion. These include changes in facial expression, noises, and body movements, such as moving legs as if riding a bicycle.

Arms: outstretched with moving fingers

Eyes: eyebrows lowered at outer edges, looking at object causing excitement

Mouth: raised corners and open in a smile

AMAZING BUT TRUE!

Sounds of emotions

Researchers studying newborn babies discovered that their brains are tuned in to human voices and the sounds of emotions. The part of babies' brains processing sounds was more active when they heard human voices than when they heard toys splashing in the bath, for example. Newborn babies respond and will turn their head towards their mothers' voice more than any other – this is a sound they have heard during pregnancy, and so it is the most familiar to them. The brain centres that control emotions were more active when the babies heard sad sounds, such as crying, than neutral ones.

Pregnant women and partners or family sometimes talk gently to babies in the weeks before they are born. They may also play soothing music. They believe this calms the baby and helps it recognize its family's voices, although there is no scientific evidence to prove that this is true.

Bonding with adults

Babies who are a few months old may smile at all sorts of people. This is called a social smile. But from around six months, babies mostly smile at their parents or particular caregivers. They may make strong eye contact and wait for a smile in response. These are parts of the process of **attachment**. Through attachment, babies establish strong and long-lasting emotional bonds with their close caregivers. They also learn that their behaviour and emotions can affect the behaviour and emotions of others.

Mutual attachment

Attachment has benefits both for babies and their parents or caregivers. It establishes the close bonds that give emotional security to each person.

Parents and close caregivers are critical for a baby's survival. They provide what the baby needs to feel safe and secure, such as food and drink, warmth, cuddles, and medicine. They play with the baby and teach him or her about the world, such as what is safe to eat or touch. By being in close contact with the emotional responses of adults, babies can learn how to respond emotionally themselves (see the studies on page 19).

Attachment is also important for parents and caregivers in holding families and societies together, so that they can support and care for each other. Babies seem demanding but they are just learning how to respond to the world around them.

It is important to respond constructively to babies. They cannot understand every word we say, but they certainly do respond to the human voice and learn to have "conversations" long before they can talk. A baby wants attention not to be selfish, but rather because attention is essential for the baby to develop healthily.

Objects of fear

New emotion: fear

Babies start to experience fear from around four months old as a response to new, unexpected, confusing, or threatening things. This is because, by this age, they can more easily remember what they have encountered before, such as distress when their parent left them alone. But exactly what they fear changes as they get older. In general, babies feel less fear when the target of their attachment is present, even in unfamiliar places or situations.

4–6 months

Unusual occurrences

For example: Speech with no visible face speaking

7–10 months

Stranger anxiety

For example: When adults who are not their parents or caregivers come close or try to pick them up

12 months

Separation anxiety

For example: When parents leave the baby, usually somewhere unfamiliar

The right environment

Emotional development throughout life, but especially in the early years, relies in part on routine and a positive environment. A framework of events that happen in a particular order each day, such as bath time and being told a story after the evening meal, provide stability and regular opportunities to experience positive emotions. Routines are important both for babies and caregivers. For example, without a sleep routine, both baby and mother will be tired and less able to cope emotionally with each other. But different babies may have different routines, because they have different needs in terms of how much they need to sleep or feed.

Pre-school and emotions

The emotional skills we build up from birth are strongly influenced by the support we receive from parents, caregivers, and our peers. Attachment is the basis upon which positive relationships with caregivers, teachers, and peers are built. For example, children who are content, positive, and confident in their abilities may do better at classroom tasks and cooperate better with other children. Therefore, they often achieve better academic results and have greater satisfaction with school.

Many studies have been carried out on groups of young children that try to measure the impact of good pre-school experiences on their emotional security when they grow up. Here are summaries of two of these studies.

Learning to play and share

Most babies and toddlers need to learn how to play with others. The support a baby gets in this process may depend on many things, such as how well educated their parents are or whether they can afford good child care when they are not around. Skills learned through play, such as how to share, reach goals, and communicate effectively, are important for emotions felt in later life.

US study

From 1969 to 1975, the Syracuse University Family Development Research Program provided emotional and practical support for 100 children between the ages of 6 and 60 months and their families in New York state, in the United States. The programme involved high-quality, daily child care with weekly home visits and parent group meetings. An equivalent group of children from the same area, whose families had similar levels of income and lived in similar homes, received no organized pre-school help. When the children were 13 to 16 years old, it was found that four times as many had been in trouble with the law in the non-programme group than the programme group, and their crimes were usually more severe and repeated.

Jamaica study

In 1990, in Jamaica, scientists started an experiment on 127 children between the ages of 9 and 24 months. Half the children started to have home visits from scientists lasting one hour, and half had no assistance. During a home visit, scientists encouraged mothers to talk to and praise their children during play. They taught the women to reinforce positive things the children did, even when they were naughty, rather than use physical punishments. They supplied the women with toys and picture books and encouraged them to play with their children between visits, too. When the children had reached 17 or 18 years old in 2006, scientists tested their emotional responses. They found that those children who had had home visits grew up to experience less anxiety and depression and better **self-esteem** than those who had not had the home visits.

AMAZING BUT TRUE!

Staying in school

The Jamaica study found that children who had had home visits were five times less likely to be expelled from school than those without the pre-school assistance. Home visits also had a big impact on how well the children did in school. Those whose families had been helped to encourage learning and to reward achievements concentrated better while learning than children who had not received this help.

Preparing for later life

Teenagers got into trouble less if they had effective pre-school assistance when babies or toddlers. The left-hand chart shows that 6 per cent of children from families taking part in the Syracuse University Program pre-school had problems with the law years later. Without this early support, 22 per cent of children (see right-hand chart) from similar backgrounds had emotional difficulties leading to arrests and time spent in correctional facilities.

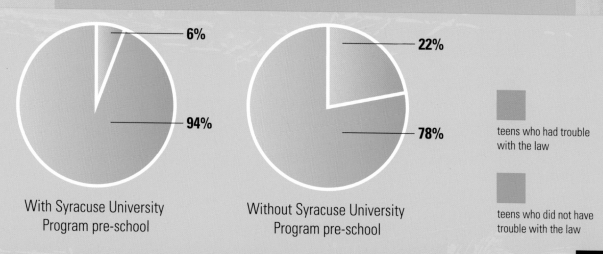

6%

94%

22%

78%

With Syracuse University Program pre-school

Without Syracuse University Program pre-school

teens who had trouble with the law

teens who did not have trouble with the law

Developing and mastering skills

As babies grow into toddlers, they learn many new skills and become more independent of their parents and caregivers. For example, they learn to walk and talk, to feed themselves, and use the toilet. Developing and mastering skills can be frustrating, especially when parents and caregivers can do them easily, but babies gain self-esteem in trying and perfecting skills. One individual's ability to learn and perfect skills may be very different from another's. For example, babies with regular ear infections may struggle to perfect skills involving balance that other babies can do easily, and they may become very frustrated as a result.

Typical emotional development during the first three years

This table outlines some of the key changes to emotions in the first years after birth.

Birth–1 year

birth–3 months
- shows a range of emotions through smiles, frowns, body movements, and gurgling
- shows attachment – recognizes and smiles at familiar people
- comforted by food and cuddles

4–6 months
- expresses joy through laughter and happy sounds
- starts to show fear of unknown people
- comforted when picked up and by hearing familiar voices

6–12 months
- expresses a wider range of emotions, including fear and sadness
- shows strong fear, uncertainty, or anxiety about strangers and clings to a parent
- comforted by thumb sucking or a familiar toy

1–2 years
- starts to say "no" and refuse naps or some foods
- feels afraid of being apart from a caregiver
- begins to understand games involving taking turns

2–3 years
- commonly has temper tantrums
- is afraid of the dark and loud noises such as trains
- shows anxiety at separation from parents or caregivers and less fear of strangers

"Terrible twos"

Around the age of two, most toddlers start to become more difficult to deal with. This is the period when they first have battles of will with parents over choosing what activities they want to do. Typically, toddlers of this age will use the word "no" a lot to test the caregiver's authority, for example, in putting away a favourite toy because it is time to eat or sleep. They also experience intense periods of rage called temper tantrums. The "terrible twos" happen during a period when children are rapidly learning words. They can become very frustrated by not being able to express how they are feeling or what they want to do using words. These periods of anger and conflict usually become less frequent as children gain language skills.

Temper tantrums

During a temper tantrum, children may cry, scream, or shout. They may hit, kick, or bite people and break or throw things. Parents or caregivers can stop tantrums from happening by distracting children with a new toy or activity, or by giving them a choice over something simple, such as which fruit they would like to eat. Once a tantrum is in full swing, the best thing is to put children somewhere where they cannot hurt themselves and leave them to get over it.

Young children may also have tantrums caused by other frustrations, such as hearing difficulties, learning difficulties, or feeling sick. Parents or caregivers need to look out for signs of other causes of tantrums in their children, such as a temperature when ill, and consult a medical professional if they are concerned.

Childhood:
four to ten years old

Childhood is when most young people start to spend more time away from their parents and caregivers. It is a period when individuals start to understand their own emotions better, understand or expect the emotional responses of others, and see the link between the two.

School

Most children go to school when they are four or five years old. They spend a large chunk of their day with their peers and a new range of adults, which is a new experience for many children. Children often feel a mix of emotions at this change in their routine, ranging from anxiety and confusion about the demands of school life, to great enjoyment at learning new skills themselves.

For many children, this stage in their lives may also bring other emotional changes, for example, as a result of moving or the arrival of a new sibling. Some emotional responses to siblings can include pleasure in having a new playmate in the house and pride at being an older, more able member of the family. But they can also include jealousy at parents' attention being divided or disappointment that the brother or sister cannot do much yet.

Social network

Most children establish a wider social network of friends, peers, and adults other than their parents when they start school. They are usually exposed to a wider range of emotional responses to deal with than ever before.

Emotions of the playground

On the playground, children learn more about their own emotions and those of others through games. The ways children initiate and take part in games, agree or disagree on roles and rules, and react to success and failure are important learning experiences they will take forward into the rest of their lives.

Playing around

Play is a very important aspect of childhood that enhances development in many ways. For example, pushing toy shopping trolleys or skipping both improve strength and coordination. While playing games, children practise language, solve problems, and develop strategies. Play also enhances emotional development. Children playing team games have to learn to trust each other and work together. They learn to become less selfish and to support other team members when things do not go well. Children may also take turns to lead the group. All of these skills are essential practice runs for adult life, from having loving, sharing relationships, to dealing with tricky dynamics in groups.

AMAZING BUT TRUE!

Screen time

A 2011 study of children between the ages of 5 and 16 in the UK found that, on average, they spent four and a half hours a day in front of a computer or television, watching films, searching the internet, and playing video games. This is more than the average four hours per week that children spend exercising outside. Exercise stimulates the brain to produce **endorphins**, which are chemicals that reduce stress and make people feel more positive.

Some screen activities can have emotional benefits for children. For example, after playing games such as *Lemmings*, which involve helping characters to survive or succeed at tasks, children were more likely to help others. However, after repeatedly playing violent games, children are more likely to be aggressive and confrontational, and sometimes they do less well in school.

Understanding oneself

Spending time with other children and adults is important in helping children become aware of their abilities, qualities, and emotional framework. When four- to six-year-old children are asked to describe themselves, they respond in terms of observable characteristics. For example, they may give hair colour or height and perhaps state their favourite colour or animal. After a few years of being in school, children are more likely to describe themselves in terms of their abilities relative to others, such as being good at running or playing the guitar. **Self-awareness** grows as a consequence of interactions with others. This is because, in order to contribute to and empathize with a group, children need to be aware of and value their own feelings and needs.

Self-image

People start to have a definite self-image for the first time in their lives as children. Children's view of what they are like and how others see them is based on the positive and negative emotions they feel about what they do.

Ages 4–5:

Recognize their own feelings

Ages 6–7:

Aware that others have different perspectives or feelings from their own

Ages 8–9:

Recognize that others can become aware of their point of view

Age 10:

Can consider the emotional impacts of social interactions both from their own and other people's points of view

Developing feelings

This timeline charts the significant changes in children's understanding of their own and others' feelings from ages 4 to 10.

Controlling emotions

Children also need to be aware of how their emotions affect others. When they are in a group or class, children will encounter situations in which they would rather rebel and do their own thing, rather than the task set by the teacher. For instance, they might feel happier whispering to the child next to them rather than sitting quietly. **Self-regulation** is when children are able to control their behaviour. They learn to follow directions, even if they don't really want to. Self-regulating also involves stopping themselves from doing the things they really do want to do.

In general, the level of self-regulation children show is linked to how well they do in school. For example, a child who cannot self-regulate at the age of five will often struggle to follow a teacher's instructions or concentrate on a task when they are seven. There is even a link between poor self-regulation when young and bullying others when older.

Scientists have found that self-regulation is linked to how the forebrain develops connections during early years of schooling. A child's brain generally has the connections between brain centres to self-regulate but it takes practice. When children practise doing things deliberately or on purpose, rather than just on impulse, the connections are gradually reinforced.
If they don't practise self-regulation, they may lose the connections and could end up having temper tantrums when things don't go their way in later life!

A new emotion: guilt

Guilt is an emotion that involves feeling bad about something that was said or done in the past. Guilt can be positive if it helps people do things better in the future, for example, avoiding teasing someone who got really upset about being teased last time. But guilt is also negative and can crush confidence about what people plan to do.

Guilt first emerges as a strong emotion during early childhood, because it is then that people understand that they could have chosen not to do something that was wrong and had negative effects on others. Some parents may accidentally encourage guilt to get their own way. For example, parents may pretend to cry to demand a hug from a child who cannot stand seeing them upset. In extreme cases, when children feel too much guilt, the feeling can turn to shame and severely affect how they interact with others.

Emotional character

What is your **temperament** like? Every one of us has an individual, basic mood that makes us respond emotionally in certain ways when faced with new or difficult challenges or situations. This basic mood is what we call our temperament. Children's temperaments are partly determined by brain chemistry inherited from their parents, such as a well-developed hypothalamus, and partly by emotional treatment and other aspects of the environment they grow up in.

Temperaments vary between two extremes. A small proportion of children are inhibited. In general they tend to be shy, timid, and restrained when faced with something new. The new challenge typically sets off fear responses, for example their heart beats faster, and there is greater activity on the right side of their brain – the side that is linked to negative emotions. At the other extreme, some children are uninhibited. These children are usually much more sociable, fearless, outgoing, and confident when faced with new situations. Most children have temperaments somewhere between these two extremes.

Emotional problems

Some children have unusual, negative patterns of behaviour and emotional responses, which result from difficulties in their lives. There are many causes of these emotional problems, and children with some temperaments are affected more by these causes than others. These include bullying (see the box on the next page), neglect, and abuse. Neglect is when children may have poor hygiene or dress because their caregivers are unwilling or unable to care for them properly, perhaps because they are dealing with serious problems of their own. Abuse is persistent and severe bad treatment by emotional, verbal, or physical (hitting or sexual) means.

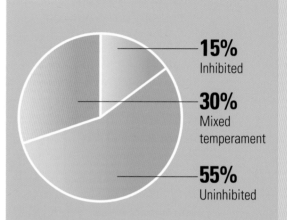

15%
Inhibited

30%
Mixed temperament

55%
Uninhibited

Temperament extremes

This pie chart shows the proportions of children with different temperaments in a group. So in an average class of twenty, about three children will be inhibited. Temperament is fixed for some children at an early age. For example, half of children classed as inhibited at the age of two are still inhibited at the age of eight.

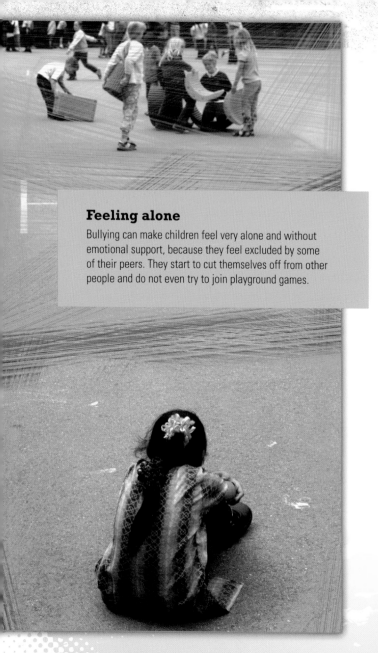

Bullying

Bullying, neglect, or abuse almost always reduces a child's confidence and self-esteem. They make children feel unwanted, unsafe, and undervalued. These powerful feelings often persist during their adult lives, too. Children find it difficult to express their feelings in words, so they may express them in other ways, such as bed wetting or pulling out their hair. Some children turn those feelings inward and become anxious, withdrawn, fearful, and uncommunicative. Others let the feelings out in a negative way, by being disobedient, breaking things, and getting into fights. The challenge for child care experts, teachers, and parents is to spot patterns that suggest emotional problems, as opposed to one-time incidents that may just be extreme emotional displays.

AMAZING BUT TRUE!

Bullying in the United Kingdom

Bullying is quite common in UK schools. The 2010–11 Tellus4 survey by the Department of Education reported that just under 29 per cent of children (Years 6, 8, and 10) are bullied in school. Victims of bullying often feel lonely, have trouble making friends, and have trouble coping with new situations or challenges. They often have low self-esteem and fear going to school. These emotions often last into adulthood and can lead to depression and other mental health problems.

The emotional impact of racism

Racism is a very specific type of bullying. It is treating people differently or unfairly based on racial or cultural differences. Racist bullying may be a response to skin colour, accent or language, general appearance from hair style to body coverings, religious beliefs or activities, or a combination of these. Myths, stereotypes, and ignorance are a big part of racism. For example, in Australia some Aboriginal people may have alcohol or aggression problems and not work, partly because of lack of opportunity and poverty. A racist view of Aboriginal people is that they are lazy drunks looking for trouble.

People from other cultures are easy targets for bullies, because they are obviously different from the majority. They are sometimes at a disadvantage, and bullies pick up on these disadvantages. For example, refugees (people who have been forced to leave their country, often for political reasons) may have the disadvantages of poorer language skills, low family income, and lack of familiarity with a place. On the next page is the story of how bullying affected Zalmai, an Afghan boy living in Australia.

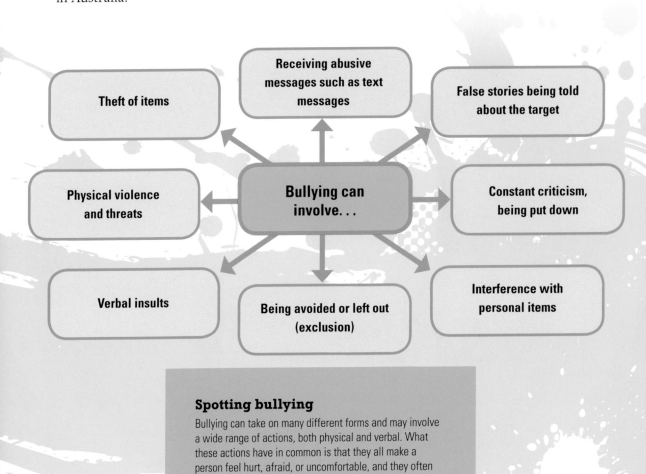

Theft of items

Receiving abusive messages such as text messages

False stories being told about the target

Physical violence and threats

Bullying can involve. . .

Constant criticism, being put down

Verbal insults

Being avoided or left out (exclusion)

Interference with personal items

Spotting bullying

Bullying can take on many different forms and may involve a wide range of actions, both physical and verbal. What these actions have in common is that they all make a person feel hurt, afraid, or uncomfortable, and they often happen more than once over a long period of time.

Case study: Zalmai's story

Zalmai's family left Afghanistan by boat to escape from conflict. Upon arrival in Australia, they lived with other Afghan refugees in a detention centre, and Zalmai went with others to school and to a language centre to learn English. He experienced racism soon after he arrived in a Melbourne suburb and started primary school there. He said: "I used to stand there and no one wanted to talk to me because I was the only Afghan. People used to sit away from me, no one wanted to be with me so I was forced to do stuff on my own. [This] affected me a lot. I felt really bad about myself. I felt like doing something about it but I couldn't."

Zalmai's family members were among the few people from Afghanistan in that community. He said: "[People] called us 'terrorist', [and said] 'go back to your country'." Afghan girls were teased for wearing the hijab (a modest style of dress that includes a scarf covering the head).

Changing perception

Many Afghan refugees faced increasing racism in Australia, as in many countries, after the 2001 terrorist attacks, carried out by a Middle Eastern terrorist group. People who had fled to Australia to escape violence and persecution in Afghanistan were suddenly perceived by many as possible terrorists because they came from the Middle East, too.

In secondary school, the bullying continued. Zalmai and his Afghan friends avoided going to the school's playing fields to play football because they were scared of the other boys playing there. At first, the bullies shouted names at Zalmai and his friends, but soon this escalated into physical abuse, with fights between the Afghan and Australian boys. Zalmai describes his emotional response, saying: "I felt put down … and felt more emotion from the inside, like anxiety and depression. I wanted to get away from that place [and have] nothing to do with it." Their school took a stand on racism and threatened expulsion to the children if they fought again, and so things settled down. The Afghan children felt more settled in school, and Zalmai said his well-being is much better.

Adolescence: ten to eighteen years old

Adolescence is the period in life between childhood and adulthood when enormous changes happen. This is the time of **puberty**, when children's bodies change into adult bodies, and these physical changes can be exciting but also stressful. Puberty also brings emotional change. Young people become more emotionally attached to their friends or boyfriends and girlfriends, and they may have to deal with emotional stress when they face important exams or have disagreements with parents or caregivers. During this period, young people learn to make more of their own choices and decisions and become more independent.

Identity

During adolescence, people start to establish a much stronger sense of identity. They can better understand and react to the world around them and become more emotionally aware. Therefore, young people get stronger ideas about what type of people they are and would like to be. **Adolescents** may make bold choices – for instance, in what they wear and their beliefs, from religion to food preferences. This is a typical aspect of changing from children, whose lives depend greatly on what is done to them, into adults, whose development involves making their own decisions. Adolescents may battle with parents, caregivers, teachers, and other figures of authority who do not approve of their identity.

Shifting identity

It is not uncommon for young people to change fashions, ideas, and even beliefs while they are searching for an identity that feels right.

Body changes

Adolescence begins with puberty, which is a physical and biological change in the body. This starts when the body begins to develop sexually. The hypothalamus causes the pituitary to release growth and **sex hormones**, causing growth spurts and the development of ovaries and testes. The ovaries make eggs and release oestrogen, causing girls to develop breasts, pubic hair, and have periods. The testes make sperm and the hormone **testosterone**, which makes boys become hairier, more muscular, and have deeper voices.

Brain growth

The brain also transforms during adolescence. It becomes more efficient at processing information. Neurons become better at making information flow faster and more widely between different brain regions. The amygdala, which is involved with processing emotions, and the **hippocampus**, which helps form memories, grow in size. These changes cause young people to think and feel differently from the way they did in childhood. For example, they think about emotions as they feel them. They also relate them better to memories and experience, so they can change and modify responses that are appropriate to the situation.

Hold that thought

Teenagers often do homework with music or the television on. This is one example of multitasking, or concentrating on several things at once. During adolescence, young people become better at multitasking because the hippocampus can hold thoughts for longer. However, the outer, front part of their brain, called the **prefrontal cortex**, is developing more slowly. This is the brain part controlling prioritization and planning. So, teenagers might be able to think of all the things they need to do at the same time, but they cannot work out which is most important to do first!

Relationships

Adolescence is the period in life when many people develop powerful relationships with their peers. Forming strong emotional bonds with peers is part of how adolescents work out their desired identity. Peers are usually going through similar biological, academic, and social changes at the same time, so they may understand the issues in each other's lives better than parents. Adolescents make strong groups of friends and increasingly spend time with them.

During puberty some adolescents begin to develop romantic – and sometimes sexual – relationships with their peers. Until recently in human history, this biological drive to reproduce was important because life was relatively short. However, in countries such as the United Kingdom, life expectancy is now around 80 years old, so people often wait to have their families later in life, in their thirties and forties. The biological drive to find a mate nevertheless still kicks in around the time of puberty.

Strong connections
The activity of sex hormones during puberty makes some adolescents seek their first sexual relationships.

AMAZING BUT TRUE!

Reading emotions

Adolescents read facial expressions differently from adults because their brains are at a different stage of development. In a 2005 study, brain researchers showed teenage and adult volunteers a series of different photos showing the facial expression of fear. All the adults recognized fear, but around 50 per cent of the teenagers read the emotion as shock, anger, or sadness.

The researchers discovered that while looking at the images, teenagers showed the most activity in their amygdala, while adults were more active in the prefrontal cortex. These findings suggest that when adolescents look at others, they may be misinterpreting the emotions other people are showing.

Uncertain times

It is natural to be uncertain about relationships, but the uncertainty is often felt very strongly by adolescents. They may become very concerned about how their friends treat them, because they are investing a lot of emotional effort in maintaining friendships. This can lead to frequent break-ups and reunions between friends.

A major reason is that physical development for some adolescents is faster than the development of their brain. They have very strong emotional responses because their inner forebrain is working more efficiently than when they were children. But the prefrontal cortex is still building up the network of links that allow them to filter their emotional responses to others. For instance, they are less able than most adults to take a critical view of the reasons why someone reacts angrily towards them. This means they are less able to avoid saying or doing things on impulse that might hurt others.

Emotions together

These people are attending the funeral of a loved one. It is easy for most teenagers to read the emotions on their faces. However, there are times when teenagers can misread emotional signals in the faces, voices, and bodies of others.

Stress

Stress comes from a very powerful set of emotions. The emotions making up stress include dread, frustration, worry, sadness, and loneliness. People feeling stress may withdraw from others and feel tense. They often experience typical fight-or-flight physical responses, including a faster heartbeat and breathing rate, cold or clammy hands and feet, and an unsettled stomach. Stress can last minutes, hours, or days.

Stressful times

Taking tests and waiting for results are big sources of stress. Not getting the right grades may not only have a big impact on future plans – it may also cause tension at home.

AMAZING BUT TRUE!

Body image

Between 50 per cent and 88 per cent of adolescent girls are unhappy with their body shape or size. This is partly a consequence of developing more body fat, especially on their hips and thighs during puberty. Studies have shown that teenage girls on average see themselves as 5.5 kilograms (11 pounds) above their ideal weight.

Boys are generally more content with their puberty changes, such as increased height and more muscular bodies, although there is more and more evidence that boys also worry about their appearance – they just say less about it! There are many reasons for body image problems, but prime among them is the idealized portrayal of people in the media, from television and magazines to the internet. For example, the average female model seen in the media is at least 15 centimetres (6 inches) taller and 14 kilograms (30 pounds) lighter than the average female looking at her.

Adolescent stress

Adolescents have many sources of stress. These include body changes, from spots to body image (see the pie chart), as well as difficulties at home, such as battles over going out with friends or parents' financial problems. They also include sexuality. Adolescents may be attracted to people of the same or opposite sex, and this may make them identify as homosexual or heterosexual.

Adolescents can reduce their stress levels in different ways. For example, exercising, listening to music, and avoiding drinking coffee or tea can all increase production of stress-busting neurotransmitters. Teenagers can learn to manage stress, too. For example, they can break down larger tasks into smaller tasks that are easier to achieve.

Sources of stress

A study of Californian teenagers revealed their main sources of stress, as shown in this pie chart. Would the pie chart look different for you and your friends?

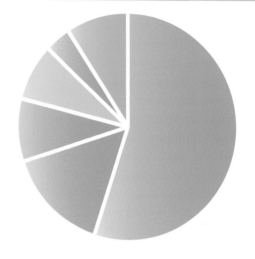

55% Homework/school
(Exams, coursework, grades and reports)

15% Parents/family
(Expectations, pressure to do well)

9% Social life
(Friends, boyfriends/ girlfriends, clubs and hobbies, auditions and shows)

8% Time
(Lack of sleep, too many activities to fit in, multitasking)

4% Sports

9% Other

Changing sleep

People feel stress more when they are tired. During adolescence, people's sleep patterns change because melatonin, a hormone that brings on sleepiness, is produced at different times than it was during childhood. This is part of the changes in the body in response to sex hormone production. Teenagers often do not feel sleepy until relatively late at night, and they sleep until later in the morning. This is rarely an issue during weekends but can make life difficult during the school week, when they need to wake up early. During a school week teenagers may build up a sleep deficit. The lack of sleep can make adolescents more emotionally fragile, and it also affects their ability to learn in school. This is because sleep is an important "time-out" for the brain to process what has happened during the day and to lay down long-term memory.

Highs and lows

Many adolescents feel as if they are riding on an emotional rollercoaster, as their moods take them up to extreme highs one day and down to extreme lows the next. These rapid changes, from elation to misery, are usually called mood swings. They are partly caused by surges in sex hormones that can act as neurotransmitters in the brain. Centres in the inner forebrain, including the amygdala and hippocampus, become more sensitive to changes in these hormone levels – and this results in sudden, large mood changes. The delay in maturity of the prefrontal cortex means that the adolescent brain is not yet able to choose what to do with these emotions.

Low moods can turn into depression. Lots of people say they are "depressed", when what they really mean is that they are feeling unhappy. Depression is a serious condition that generally involves extreme feelings of stress and sadness lasting at least two weeks or more. Anyone can get depressed, but people at special risk include those who have lost a close friend, whose parents are getting divorced, who have a history of being abused, and those with especially low self-esteem or who put a lot of academic pressure on themselves. There are many signs of depression in adolescents. These range from changes in behaviour such as avoiding friends or not attending school to extremes of behaviour including **self-harming** (see pages 38 and 39) and suicide attempts.

Brain chain

How does the brain affect teenagers' emotional responses when they are asked to clean their room? This flow chart gives an idea of the chain of events:

Trigger
When they are asked to do a task such as cleaning their room.

Response
Teenager thinks: "They're angry with me, but it's my room, not their room."

Amygdala: Neurotransmitter activity causes feelings of anger.

Hippocampus: Neurotransmitter activity activates memories of how to express anger.

Teenager says: "Get off my back about this."

Trigger
Parents say: "I'm getting angry now – just get it done or you're grounded."

Response
Teenager thinks: "It is a good idea to clean the room rather than get angry because (a) it will get my parents off my back and (b) I won't be grounded."

Hippocampus: Memories of positive emotions that have followed cleaning the room are activated.

Prefrontal cortex: Neurotransmitter activity suppresses the anger based on communication with the hippocampus.

Amygdala: Neurotransmitter activity decreases feelings of anger.

Teenager cleans room

Anger control

Adolescents can get very angry, especially when they are stressed out or depressed. Anger is not just about yelling, punching walls, and slamming doors. It also includes sulking, prejudice, sarcasm, and hurtful gossip. Adolescents are bigger, stronger, and more aware of the emotions of others than children are, so they can cause more damage and hurt to themselves and others.

Around 10 per cent of adolescents have trouble controlling their anger, and more of these are boys than girls. This is partly because one of the effects of testosterone can be to increase aggressive responses in the brain, and it is partly due to faster development in the hippocampus in boys than in girls. This brain centre controls expressions of aggression.

Dealing with anger is a skill that takes practice for many adolescents. The first step is self-awareness. People have to work out what particular things they get the angriest about. What do they feel and think as they get angry? Once people know the signs of anger welling up, they can learn self-control and think before they act. They can then consider options other than getting angry.

New emotion: PMS

During puberty, girls often start to feel moody, irritable, tearful, or tired and have difficulty concentrating. This is premenstrual syndrome, or PMS, which is both an emotion and a condition that causes the emotion. It is caused by changes in sex hormone levels before periods, which reduce amounts of serotonin in the blood. This lowers mood and energy levels.

Stress-buster

Yoga is a fun, stress-busting activity that teenagers often enjoy. It not only works the body to reduce tension in muscles and joints, but it can also distract people from thinking about their sources of stress.

Self-harming

Self-harming is an extreme form of emotional behaviour, but it is not that unusual. In a study of 2,000 adolescents, it was found that around 1 in 10 teenagers self-harm and that more of these are girls than boys. The people who self-harm often suffer from depression and may also drink alcohol or take drugs. The most common ways that teenagers self-harm are by self-cutting and burning, but other methods include poisoning with medicines, such as drug overdoses, and punching themselves or banging their heads against walls. This practice is very dangerous. Apart from the effects of drug overdoses or loss of blood, self-harming can cause infections and sometimes paralysis if people damage their nerves.

Harm to calm

A self-harmer, Helena, describes her self-harming like this: "It wasn't the sensation of the pain itself but the body's reaction. It was a kind of numbed feeling. When I hurt myself I felt I completely calmed down, my mind focused on the pain and the wound."

True or false?

There are many misconceptions about self-harming. What is true and what is false?

1. *People who self-harm are just doing it to get attention.*

    This is false. Self-harmers do it mainly to cope with or escape from painful emotions they are feeling.

2. *People who self-harm do it because they feel like they want to commit suicide.*

    This is mostly false. Self-harming is a way to deal with intense emotions, not a suicide attempt. However, some people who self-harm may be at greater risk of suicide if their self-harming goes untreated for a long time.

3. *People who self-harm do it to relieve intense emotions.*

    This is true. Some people say that when they feel more physical pain, they feel less emotional pain.

Self-harming can be treated and cured. An important step is to talk to someone about it. Teenagers may not feel comfortable opening up even to close friends, but they may do so to a teacher or school counsellor, a doctor, or a trusted family member. By talking through the feelings that lead to the self-harm and dealing with them, many people are able to stop self-harming. There are also confidential organizations that can help people who self-harm.

Changing harm

This graph illustrates how in the study of 2,000 teenagers the average proportion of self-harming individuals changed with their age. Most of the adolescents started self-harming before they were 16, but a lower percentage were self-harming at the age of 17 and a half.

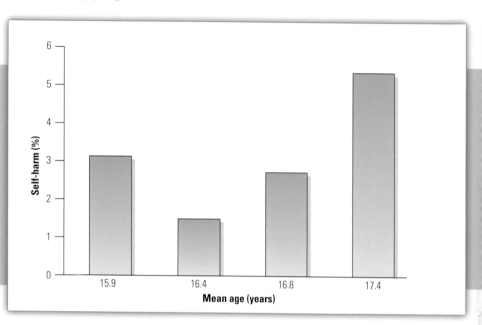

Case study: Jennifer's story

"Have you ever been so angry that you want to scream? Well, that is what it's like, it's a way of screaming in silence." This is what Jennifer said she felt when she first harmed herself as a child. "I remember the first time so clearly. I was feeling really wound up and angry and just stood and pulled a chunk of my hair out. I liked the sensation it gave me. I felt the hair coming out but didn't feel any pain. It is the strangest thing and very hard to explain, but it was like all the pressure that I had been feeling was coming out at that moment. I was so surprised that it didn't hurt and soon started scratching myself with my nails as well."

By the time she was a teenager, self-harming was part of her daily routine. She cut herself with razor blades and hid her scars by wearing long-sleeved tops. "Over time it evolved into how deep the cut was and how much blood came out," she said. Jennifer was very depressed as a result of bullying. She remembers: "I used to wake up in my room in the morning with cuts on me and not even remember doing it. I'd always feel really guilty and upset afterwards. I do it to cope with everyday life. When you are in the grip of it ... nothing else matters until you cut."

Risky behaviour

Adolescents sometimes put themselves at risk. They do so partly because natural chemicals such as endorphins are released during some risky activities, which can make them feel good and block out feelings of stress. It is also partly because their brains are incapable of making all the safest choices. Here are a few risky behaviours found in adolescents:

- *Taking drugs*: Drugs harm people physically – for example, by making their heart beat too fast. They also affect the way brain neurons send, receive, and process information. This alters the user's perception of reality and can cause deep lows in emotions and moods, making the person more likely to take other risks.

- *Unprotected sex*: Sex without a condom increases the chance not only of pregnancy but also of catching sexually transmitted diseases (STDs).

- *Dangerous stunts*: Adolescents sometimes do dangerous things, such as driving too fast or aggressively, to impress their friends. Dangerous stunts are incredibly risky.

Adrenaline rush

Doing a stunt like this is scary but exciting – a sudden feeling of fear releases lots of adrenaline, a hormone that makes people feel good.

AMAZING BUT TRUE!

Driving risks

A 2011 study tested the risk-taking behaviour of adolescents and adults using a realistic driving video game. The aim was to drive a route as quickly as possible. When they played individually, adolescents performed in a similar way to adults. But when playing in a group with their peers, adolescents ran through yellow and red traffic lights to save time more often than the adults. This risk-taking happens in reality, too. Teenagers in groups are five times more likely to be in a car accident than when driving alone.

Peer pressure

Being part of a peer group can have a positive effect on behaviour and emotions. For example, talking to other teenagers about problems with parents can help put young people's own problems into perspective. But it can also have a negative effect. Peers can exert a great emotional pressure on each other to do things they should not or do not want to do, such as have sex before they are ready to or before it is legal. Teenagers may make reluctant peers feel the anxiety of being outside the group, or even tease reluctant peers about not being grown up enough to take part in forbidden or risky behaviour.

AMAZING BUT TRUE!

Gang warfare

Being part of a gang gives people powerful emotions of belonging and loyalty, but there are also feelings of fear, anxiety, and guilt, which result from the violence that is often part of gang life. There are nearly 800,000 teenagers in as many as 30,000 gangs in the United States. Although in some places this is only around 14 per cent of the total number of teenagers, gang members are responsible for nearly 50 per cent of violent crimes. Some teenagers think that joining a gang helps to protect them from violence from bullies in other gangs, but in reality a gang member is 60 times more likely to be killed violently than an average person.

Ganging up

Teenagers have a strong emotional need to be part of a peer group. Gang membership is the most extreme form of this.

Adulthood

Adulthood is a very long stage in life that begins after the final phase of adolescence and ends with death. Obviously, huge emotional changes and demands can happen through those decades, but the period can be broken up into three stages characterized by different emotional demands: early adulthood, middle age, and old age. This chapter will look at emotions in the period before old age.

Early adulthood

Young adults – in their late teens, twenties, or early thirties – have learned many of the emotional skills they need to face two typical challenges of early adulthood. The first is having an emotionally close, intimate, loving relationship with another person. This partner may be part of an adolescent friendship group or someone they meet in a new situation, such as going to university or starting work. Getting to know a partner involves empathy – becoming sensitive to and understanding another person's emotional responses. For this new relationship to succeed, people often need to be less self-centred than they were as adolescents and be able to comfort and improve their partner's mood.

The second challenge in early adulthood is becoming fully independent of parents or caregivers. This is when many people start to be self-sufficient, providing their own food, clothing, and housing – usually by working for money. Many people in this age group will finish studying and then start and establish careers. They will often move out from the family home, either with a partner, with friends, or on their own. This big change can bring people happiness and pride at taking full control of their social life and making their home as they like it. It can also bring great anxiety – for example, over earning enough money to pay bills.

Family dynamics

The more people there are in a family, the wider the range of emotional demands there will be on each other. It is challenging but fun to balance their different needs, so that everyone feels happy.

Becoming a parent

Many couples choose to start families after forming a strong bond and living in their own home. This is the start of an intense emotional journey. During pregnancy, changes in hormone levels can cause many women to have highs and lows of emotion in anticipation of the birth. Many experience the strongest joy they have ever felt upon seeing their child after the birth, but 10 per cent of women become depressed after birth (see the box on the right).

One of the emotional difficulties of parenthood is finding the right balance of life and work. This means spending enough time with a child to develop strong emotional bonds while also handling the demands of a job, which might require working late or travelling away from the family for extended periods of time.

A new emotion: Postnatal depression

Postnatal depression is a long-term illness and mood in some women that usually develops within a few months after giving birth. Women feel irritated, completely exhausted, unable to enjoy anything, anxious about the health of the baby, and guilty about not being able to cope. It is a consequence both of changing hormone levels and stress about being a perfect parent.

Rewards and demands of parenthood

Balancing act

Becoming a parent creates many positive and negative emotions to deal with. Balancing the different emotions changes over time as new parents learn skills and see how other parents cope. This graphic shows just a few of the conflicting emotions.

Rewards

- Sharing the development of children with a partner
- Love and affection of children
- Development of a unique relationship
- Excitement at seeing a baby do new things
- Bringing pleasure to the family
- Learning parenting skills

Demands

- Frustration at feeling incompetent
- Stress of responsibility
- Conflicting demands of baby and partner/friends
- Anxiety over whether the baby is developing normally
- Feeling exhausted and unable to cope
- Frustration that life is completely dominated by the baby

Later adulthood

During their forties and fifties, the emotional demands for many adults have shifted. Many are established in their careers and may have more money than when they were younger. They also have more leisure time, as their children are starting to leave home. Some use the time to become socially involved, for example, by helping out with charities. They may take up hobbies such as dance, golf, or gardening and travel more widely.

AMAZING BUT TRUE!

"Bucket lists"

People going through a midlife transition often make lists of things they want to do before they die, or "kick the bucket". A 2011 survey found that 69 per cent of Americans had such a "bucket list". The most popular items on these lists were to travel to a specific destination, to achieve a professional goal, to do something for charity, to see a particular concert or sporting event, and to do something dangerous. Popular dangerous activities included white-water rafting and skydiving.

Trip of a lifetime

These older adults are on a mountain trek. Taking a trip like this may have been a dream or plan for many years, but perhaps they were too busy caring for their children or did not have the time and money to go when they were younger.

In later adulthood, people may feel the demands of caring once more. Their own parents may have health problems and require more support, especially if one of them dies. Their children may start to have children of their own. Suddenly, there are extra demands on their time, such as spending time with grandchildren and taking parents to medical appointments. Adults may have to take a parental role in making decisions about the lives of their own parents, but feel that control over their own lives is being taken away by their children. These changes can have emotional effects such as stress and frustration.

Need for changes

Many people reevaluate their lives during middle age. This process can cause sufficient emotional turmoil in up to a quarter of people over 40 that it becomes a **midlife crisis**. There are several biological reasons for this. In women, there is the hormonal turmoil of **menopause** (see page 46), as the levels of female sex hormones die away. In men, testosterone levels may fall, but even without big hormonal changes, many men go through big emotional changes.

People may feel, for example:

- frustration at not having done things they had hoped to during their youth

- sadness at the loss of children who had been the emotional focus of many years and are now "leaving the nest"

- anxiety about gaining weight, even though it is a natural tendency of the body at this age

Different people react to these emotions in different ways. Some make simple changes to feel happier, such as dressing in clothes they think make them look younger or going to the gym. Others make more complicated life changes that cause more emotional turmoil, such as changing careers or even ending their relationship.

Midlife crisis

Middle-aged people may have more money and time to reinvent themselves, perhaps by finding a new, younger partner. This can improve self-esteem but also may cause great emotional damage, for example if people conclude that their appeal to younger partners is purely financial.

Body matters

Natural ageing processes during middle age can affect people's self-esteem and confidence. For example, adult hair starts to turn grey and thin, and it recedes or even disappears for some men. People often become less active but still eat the same amounts, which in turn leads to the appearance of extra fat on the body.

Middle-aged women also undergo menopause. This is a natural process when women gradually stop producing eggs. Menopause can take years during which periods become irregular and finally end. It causes great sadness in some women, because they cannot have children anymore. This is the case both in women who already have children and in those who have never wanted any. A decrease in sex hormones during menopause causes an increase in levels of a hormone called gonadotropin. This also has a negative emotional impact by causing hot flushes, irritability, and sweating at night.

Exercise for bones

Hormonal changes during menopause cause bones to lose density. Exercising muscles to move bones and joints can help increase bone strength. Exercise makes people feel happier, too.

AMAZING BUT TRUE!

How antidepressants work

Many doctors combat depression by using antidepressants, which increase the activity of brain neurotransmitters such as serotonin. Normally, neurotransmitters are recycled at synapses after one nerve impulse passes between neurons, so they can be used to pass on the next message. Antidepressants such as Prozac stop serotonin from being recycled, leaving higher levels in the brain and this makes people feel happier.

Depression

A combination of stresses can tip some middle-aged people into depression. These stresses include not only midlife crises and body changes, but also health problems that limit activity or work such as back pain or heart disease. People may have financial pressures such as the risk of losing their job. A 2011 survey found that over a quarter of middle-aged people in the United Kingdom suffered from anxiety and depression. Worldwide depression is one of the leading reasons why people are unable to work or take care of their daily responsibilities.

As we have seen, depression is a very low mood, and it is also an illness caused by low levels of neurotransmitters such as serotonin in the brain. In the United Kingdom alone, doctors write more than 39 million prescriptions each year for **antidepressant** drugs that can ease depression. There are many different types of antidepressants, and people respond differently to them. Many suffer side effects such as changes in blood pressure after taking these drugs. Therefore, treatment is often based on trial and error until doctors discover what works for an individual. Lifestyle changes such as increased exercise can help combat depression, but talking to supportive partners and friends and visiting a psychiatrist (an expert in treating mental illness) may have a bigger impact.

AMAZING BUT TRUE!

Fatty acids and happiness

A study in 1998 compared the rate of depression in different countries with the average amount of fish people ate. It showed that in countries where more oily fish was eaten, there were fewer cases of depression. For example, there was half as much depression in Korea, where people ate on average 50 kilograms (100 pounds) of fish, as there was in New Zealand, where people ate less than half that amount of fish. The science behind it is that omega-3 fatty acids in fish oil are important in the production of serotonin, a neurotransmitter that increases a positive mood.

Symptoms of depression

These are some of the symptoms of major depression, an illness that affects over 100 million people worldwide:

- Loss of interest in pleasurable activities
- Changes in appetite resulting in weight gain or loss
- Sleepless nights or oversleeping
- Feeling restless or irritable
- Feeling worthless or guilty
- Difficulty in concentrating or making decisions

Old age

An adult does not wake up one day and realize he or she has reached old age. Growing older is a lifelong process.

For many, old age is a time at the end of adulthood when they can look back over their lives. Many older adults will have retired from work, and their children will usually be parents or even grandparents. Some people look back with happiness and contentment that their lives had meaning, such as raising families and having good careers, and that they have contributed fully to life and society.

Others feel intense despair in old age. They may fear the approaching end of their life because the unknown can be frightening, and because they feel their past has been wasted. Alternatively, they may think they have found all the right answers, but they feel despair because they believe that other people's opinions, such as how to run society, are worthless.

Body impacts

Older people's outlooks on life's journey are partly the result of their temperament and also changing feelings during old age. Some of these are the consequence of changes to their bodies. In general, older people have slower reaction times and worse motor coordination. Their eyesight, hearing, attention span, and reactions generally worsen. This can cause great frustration, particularly when trying to read books or listen to conversations, or when trying to operate technology such as computers, mobile phones, or televisions. Older people may feel great sadness at losing their independence when they become unable to drive safely or become more uncertain about getting public transport, being in crowded places, or crossing roads.

AMAZING BUT TRUE!

More elderly people

In 2011, around 1 in 10 people globally was over 60 years old, but by 2050 it is predicted that this ratio will be 1 in 5. With the global population predicted to reach nearly 10 billion, that means there will be 2 billion older people. By then, there will be more older people than there are children between the ages of birth and 14. The average age that people will reach will be over 80 in many countries. This is quite a contrast to Roman times, when old age was rare and the average life expectancy was just 25 years! The transformation in the ages we reach is the result of improved health care and diet.

Health difficulties can become a major source of frustration for some older people. For example, they may have bone fractures or breaks because their bones become less dense following hormonal changes such as menopause. Their joints (such as knees) may become stiff and they may suffer from arthritis, a disease that makes the joints of the body swollen and painful. Older people often take longer to recover from illnesses. Older people may also have to cope with their emotional responses to changes in appearance such as losing hair and teeth, developing more wrinkled skin, and shrinking in height.

Learning to walk again

Many older people need to have their hips or knees replaced after they break joints or have severe joint pain. They may then experience the joy of walking or walking without pain again, rather than the challenges of not being able to get around by themselves.

Social impacts

For most people, ageing brings more leisure time. This gives many people a chance to spend more time with friends and to do the things they like to do. Many older people feel more socially confident than they did when they were younger. But some are limited in their social interaction by money issues. For example, reduced pensions (payments made to retired people) in many countries and a rising cost of living are making older people poorer. Many older people feel anxiety about being out of step with modern society. They may feel threatened by dangers they perceive in the modern environment, such as speeding cars, reliance on computers, and the presence of young people out at night on the streets. Many older people feel others do not notice them because they are too old to be socially useful, now that they have stopped working and their children have grown up.

Global ageing survey

A survey carried out by HelpAge International in 2011 offered some interesting insights into older people's lives across the globe. The survey was based on responses to questions asked by HelpAge workers and volunteers, answered by 1,265 people over 60 from 32 countries across Africa, Asia, Eastern Europe, Western Europe, and the Caribbean.

A better place?: 48 per cent thought the world is becoming a better place, 15 per cent thought it is staying the same, and 29 per cent think it is getting worse for older people.

Enough to live on?: 72 per cent said their income, from the state and from work, does not pay for sufficient water, electricity, food or decent housing.

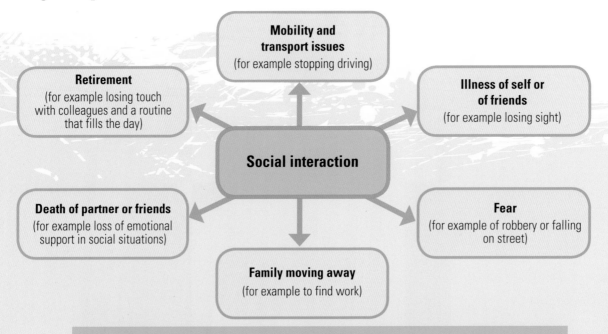

Mobility and transport issues (for example stopping driving)

Retirement (for example losing touch with colleagues and a routine that fills the day)

Illness of self or of friends (for example losing sight)

Social interaction

Death of partner or friends (for example loss of emotional support in social situations)

Fear (for example of robbery or falling on street)

Family moving away (for example to find work)

Life changes

There are many changes that can affect the lives of older people and impact upon their emotions and moods. Many are concerned with ease of getting around, changes in networks of friends and family, and changes to daily routines. There are also life changes in society or neighbourhood, for example, when the area they have lived in for many years has an influx of new, unfamiliar people.

Nursing homes

In very old age, people increasingly need others to help care for them. Some move into sheltered accommodation, which are homes with a warden or other assistance available on site. Almost everyone takes time to adjust to the new setting. At its most positive, this step is a rich experience where people can build satisfying relationships with others. At its most negative, it can make older people feel, for example, disorientated at living in a new place and embarrassed that they need strangers to help them deal with conditions such as incontinence (the inability to control the bladder and bowels).

People's emotions in a nursing home depend in part on their mental health. For example, one-third of people over 95 in the United Kingdom have a form of **dementia** (see pages 52 to 53) such as **Alzheimer's disease**. Dementia is when parts of the brain stop working properly, causing symptoms such as loss of memory, changes in mood, and problems communicating.

Staying active

Although many older people suffer from health issues, others remain very physically active. They may move more slowly and have less strength than before, but their activity can give great emotional satisfaction.

AMAZING BUT TRUE!

Age changes brains

When people get older, their brains change physically. Spaces in the brain enlarge, grooves on the brain surface deepen, and the brain shrinks slightly. Most scientists believe these changes are caused when neurons die and are not replaced by new ones. Dead neurons and chemicals such as proteins can form hard tangles and clumps through the ageing brain. When these tangles and clumps form in certain brain centres, they can prevent activity and damage healthy neurons, causing brain disorders. For example, people with Alzheimer's disease have many clumps in their hippocampus, a centre responsible for long term memory. Ageing people are more at risk of having strokes, too. These are interruptions in blood supply to the brain, causing neuron death; they often happen in older people, because their blood vessels get thinner. The physical and emotional impact of a stroke varies depending on which brain parts are affected.

Living with dementia

Dementia has a huge impact on people's lives and emotions. Brain changes for people with dementia affect how they experience the world around them and how they react to it. As a result, most show changes in how they feel and express emotions that can be short-lived or more long-term.

Some people with dementia feel very frightened because they cannot work out where they are or whom they are speaking to. Others feel very anxious and may fidget, be unable to sit still, keep asking questions, or frequently call relatives. People with dementia may become very suspicious of others, such as accusing people of stealing things they have themselves misplaced or even hidden. Others get very angry and sometimes violent. Dementia affects brain functioning, but it does not necessarily affect memory: some people with dementia have amazingly accurate memories.

Connecting
Caregivers can find working with people with dementia very rewarding, as long as they establish personal connections.

Case study: Kathy's story

Caregivers may experience a wide range of different emotions and mental abilities in older people with dementia. Some people with dementia are highly social, but many are withdrawn and difficult to relate to.

Kathy volunteered at a women's nursing home in New York, hoping to make a difference in the residents' lives. She said: "I am helping men and women who are three, four, and even five times my age, to accomplish basic tasks." Kathy looked forward to helping them, but she could not easily connect with the residents, saying: "About half of the women sat … staring vacantly into space. The other ladies … talked about the past as if it were the present; however, recent events such as lunch and today's activities were lost memories." She found that some residents liked "to hold stuffed animals and baby dolls as well. They would sometimes talk to the toys. It unnerved me at first to hear grown people talking to baby dolls as if the toys were alive."

Kathy found that people opened up more to her when they felt reassured. She held their hand and smiled at them. She also found that residents felt less stressed and more connected if she had simpler expectations of what they could achieve. She says: "I had been expecting them to relate to me on my terms instead of the other way around. My expectations had put a distance between us; once I came to this understanding, I was able to communicate and connect with the residents in a new way."

AMAZING BUT TRUE!

Seeing things

Some people with dementia experience vivid hallucinations. Some people mistake what they see, such as imagining that a chest of drawers is a toilet. Others believe they can see things that are not really there, such as strange shapes, distorted faces, animals, and landscapes. Scientists believe that dying or abnormal neurons in the amygdala and around the hippocampus distort memories in people with dementia. Their brains process what they see as these distorted versions of reality.

Family support

Do your grandparents have lots of pictures of family in their homes? Families are very important in the emotional well-being of most older people. Families provide a sense of security, from helping with essential tasks such as shopping for food to companionship during holidays. In some cases, older people move in with their children and grandchildren. In others, grandparents may act as the main caregivers of their grandchildren. For example, the parents may be ill, away on business trips, or unable to afford other child care. In the UK, there are around 14 million grandparents who together provide child care worth nearly £4 billion each year.

Grandchildren often find spending time with grandparents and other older people to be very emotionally rewarding. For example, teenagers with stresses in their lives may be able to talk to their grandparents more easily than to their parents. Grandparents have the wisdom brought by long life experience, and they are not in daily conflict with teenagers about how to manage their life. Spending time with grandchildren also helps older people understand what life is like for the younger generation today. Grandchildren may even be able to help their grandparents to use computers and other modern technology.

Emotional perspective

Grandparents can often bring a new perspective to things for young people – and even help them have more sympathy for their parents! They can help grandchildren understand how their parents and other people in their lives feel and why they behave as they do.

New emotions: grief

An inevitable side of getting old is that more of older people's peers, including those they are close to, will die. People may feel the emotion of grief at any time in their lives, but older people may have to get used to it as a regular occurrence. Grief is not just felt at the loss of a person, but also other, related things. For example, people might feel a sense of loss about future activities such as theatre and shopping trips when the friend with whom they did those activities dies, or they might feel the loss of shared experiences from the past when someone close to them dies. But as with many emotional responses, the more it is repeated, the less powerful it is, and so grief can become easier to bear with age. And the feeling of grief about a lost loved one may be less intense if the loved one was older and lived a full life than if the person was younger.

Emotional rollercoaster

The emotions we feel throughout our lives can take us from deep lows to extreme highs. This emotional rollercoaster is a journey that is essential to understanding ourselves and others.

Changing emotions through life

As we have seen, the biological and social changes that happen to individuals throughout their lives have enormous effects on their emotions. Bonding with parents and caregivers, developing independence, forming strong bonds with peers and friends, leaving home, finding a partner, raising families, and coping with the life changes in middle and older age are very important milestones in the emotional journey.

Quiz

Find out how much you remember about the changing emotions we feel throughout our lives by completing this quiz. You will find the answers on page 63.

1. Emotions last longer than moods.

   True or false?

2. Which of the following is a centre in the forebrain involved in how we feel emotions?

   a) amygdala   b) adrenal gland   c) hypothalamus

3. The left side of the brain cortex establishes positive emotions and the right side establishes negative emotions.

   True or false?

4. People feel happier when they have low levels of serotonin in the brain.

   True or false?

5. The fight-or-flight response, which happens when we are nervous, causes physical symptoms such as a faster heart rate, dilated pupils, and sweating.

   True or false?

6. Attachment is the way an infant clings onto his or her mother or main caregiver.

   True or false?

7. What is a baby's social smile?

   a) a deliberate smile while looking at an adult
   b) a smile made when a baby sees a toy
   c) a smile made only at parties

8. At what age is a toddler likely to have temper tantrums?

   a) birth–1 year   b) 2–3 years   c) 4–5 years

9. On average, children in the United Kingdom spend more time exercising outside than they do watching TV and other screen-based activities.

    True or false?

10. Which of the following is NOT a cause of stress in teenagers?

    a) tests   b) arguing with parents   c) exercise

11. Self-harming can be a violent act, but people do it so that they can feel more calm and in control.

    True or false?

12. What is a midlife crisis?

    a) an emergency that happens in middle age, like a car crash
    b) feelings of disappointment, worry, or low self-esteem during middle age
    c) hair loss after a man enters his forties

13. What percentage of the global population will be over 60 in 2050?

    a) 5 per cent   b) 20 per cent   c) 50 per cent

14. Self-awareness is awareness of one's own emotional needs and temperament and seeing how they are different from those of others.

    True or false?

Facts and figures

This section has some figures and facts relating to topics that have an impact on emotions, which were introduced earlier in the book.

Depression and poverty

How much money people have is one of the most important stress and depression life factors for adults. This bar chart shows how depression in the United States is at least twice and at most four times higher among people below the poverty level than people above it. People who live below the poverty level do not earn enough money to pay for basic needs, such as adequate food. The biggest impact of income on depression is felt among older adults between the ages of 40 and 59. Why do you think this is?

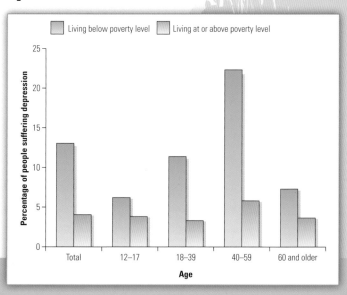

Money matters

The bar chart above summarizes a 2005–2006 study on depression and the amount of money people have. It found that over all the age groups surveyed, more than twice as many people living below the poverty level than over it suffered from depression. The biggest differences in bar heights were seen in 18–59 year olds, demonstrating that money matters for emotional well-being, especially in this age group.

Stressed out?

The following are five typical signs of stress:

- Getting irritated easily
- Being sensitive to criticism
- Biting nails
- Struggling to sleep or concentrate
- Indigestion

The following are five ways to feel better:

- Talking to others who are not too critical about how you are feeling
- Taking people up on offers of practical help
- Doing one thing at a time – don't keep piling stress upon stress
- Letting off steam in a way that causes no harm (for example, shout, scream, or hit a pillow)
- Walking away from stressful situations and taking a deep breath before reacting

Mental health

People who are mentally healthy can realize their potential, cope with the normal stresses of life, work productively and fruitfully, and make a contribution to their community. Most people manage their physical health better than their mental health. Mental health problems range from conditions such as depression, self-harm, substance abuse, and suicide, to mental disorders such as schizophrenia (a disease that makes it difficult to separate reality from fantasy), dementia, and obsessive-compulsive disorder. Mental health has social and biological causes. Here are some interesting statistics:

- About 450 million people worldwide have mental disorders.
- In the United Kingdom, an average of three children or young people in a school or college class will have mental health problems.
- Half of people surveyed with mental health issues suffered from deep anxiety and depression.

Emotional abuse

Emotional abuse is the repeated and severe bad treatment of a child that undermines the child's confidence and self-worth. Here are five types of emotional abuse:

- Ignoring a child or being repeatedly absent
- Constant criticism, humiliation, or control of a child
- Discipline through punishments that degrade the child, such as being forced to stand outside in the cold
- Exposing the child to domestic violence, substance abuse, or other distressing things
- Expecting or demanding too much of a child academically

These types of abuse can all result in problems such as:

- problems making friends or socializing in other ways
- learning difficulties
- aggressive or rebellious behaviour
- making people dislike them (self-isolation).

Glossary

abuse persistent and severe bad treatment by emotional, verbal, or physical (hitting or sexual) means

adolescence period following the start of puberty when a young person develops from a child into an adult

adolescent young person going through adolescence after puberty begins

adrenal gland small gland located on top of the kidney, which produces hormones controlling, for example, heart rate, blood pressure, and stress

adrenaline stress hormone made by the adrenal gland that is part of the fight-or-flight response

Alzheimer's disease disease of the brain where protein builds up and kills neurons. This is a form of dementia, or loss of brain function.

amygdala part of the brain that is involved with anger, anxiety, and depression

antidepressant medicine used to treat depression

attachment emotional relationship between a child and a parent or main caregiver

brain centre distinct region of the brain with a particular role, for example, in forming memories or feeling and expressing emotions

cell building blocks of living things. Cells can make energy from nutrients, reproduce, and carry out special functions, such as neurons transmitting messages in the brain.

cortex outer layer of the brain

culture way of life, customs, and social organization of a community or country

dementia serious mental condition that affects the ability to think, remember, and behave normally

depression medical condition that makes a person feel very sad, unable to cope, and without hope

empathy ability to understand another person's feelings

endorphin hormone produced in the brain that reduces feelings of pain or stress

fight or flight brain's response to a threat that prepares the body to fight or run away

forebrain large, front part of the brain, consisting of the cerebrum, thalamus, and hypothalamus.

gland organ in living things that produces fluids with particular functions in the body. For example, in mammals the breast glands secrete milk to feed the young.

hippocampus part of the brain involved in memory and emotion

hormone chemical produced by one body part to send messages that affect cells in other parts

hypothalamus part of the brain that helps control the expression of emotions, such as laughter, and also releases hormones controlling the pituitary gland

instinct way of thinking or acting that people are born with

menopause time in a woman's life when her periods stop, usually around the age of 50

midlife crisis feelings of disappointment, worry, or low self-esteem that a person may feel in the middle part of life (middle age)

neglect when children may have poor hygiene, lack of food, or inadequate clothing because their caregivers are unwilling or unable to care for them properly

neuron cell that carries information within the brain and between the brain and the rest of the body

neurotransmitter chemical that carries messages between neurons; the levels of them in the brain can affect emotions

phobia strong, unreasonable fear of something

pituitary gland gland in the brain that controls the functioning of other glands

prefrontal cortex outer, front part of the brain

puberty when a person's body gradually changes from a child's body into an adult's body

self-awareness awareness and understanding of one's own character and temperament

self-esteem person's feelings of being content with his or her character and abilities

self-harming when someone deliberately hurts himself or herself as a result of emotional problems

self-regulation when a person can control himself or herself, for example, controlling one's temper

serotonin neurotransmitter that can affect how happy a person feels

sex hormone hormone, such as oestrogen or testosterone, that affects sexual development or reproduction

stimulate make something develop or become more active

stimulus (plural: **stimuli**) thing that makes something else develop or become more active. Heat is a stimulus that causes people to move their hands away from a flame.

synapse chemical junction between two neurons controlling the flow of nerve messages

temperament tendency to react in a certain emotional way, for example, with anger

testosterone male sex hormone that makes men develop sexual characteristics such as a hairy chest

Find out more

Books

Blame My Brain: The Amazing Teenage Brain Revealed, Nicola Morgan (Walker Books, 2007)

Cool That Anger! (Life Skills), Louise Spilsbury (Heinemann Library, 2009)

Cyber Bullying (Hot Topics), Nick Hunter (Raintree, 2012)

Emotion and Relationships (Through Artists' Eyes), Jane Bingham (Raintree, 2007)

Girls' Guide to Feeling Fabulous! (Life Skills), Barbara Sheen (Heinemann Library, 2009)

Understanding Myself: A Kid's Guide to Intense Emotions and Strong Feelings, Mary C. Lamia (Magination, 2010)

Websites

www.bbc.co.uk/health/emotional_health/mental_health
Find out more about mental health on this website.

www.bbc.co.uk/science/humanbody/mind
This website provides lots of fascinating information about the mind.

www.beatbullying.org
www.bullying.co.uk
These useful sites provide help and advice on how to cope with bullying.

www.talktofrank.com/drugs-on-the-brain
Discover more about how different drugs affect your brain on this website.

Places to visit

The Science Museum
Exhibition Road
South Kensington
London SW7 2DD
www.sciencemuseum.org.uk/WhoAmI/Visit.aspx
This gallery, called "Who Am I?", covers many aspects of our self-awareness from memories and emotions to genetics.

@Bristol

Anchor Road, Harbourside, Bristol BS1 5DB

www.at-bristol.org.uk/allaboutus.html

Visit the "All About Us" interactive exhibition at this science centre. You can even see a real human brain!

Topics to research

Ageing population

The proportion of older people in the global population is rising. See www.helpage.org/resources/ageing-data/ageing-in-motion/ for a graphic showing this change since 1960. Explore the reasons for this and the likely effects. For example, the age of retirement is rising in many countries, and governments are increasingly having trouble affording pensions and care for the old. What effect will this have on emotions?

Future moods

Imagine that one day you will have a child. Write a letter of advice for that child to read when he or she reaches the age you are right now. Tell the child about the moods and emotions you experienced at this age, and how you hope your child will deal with his or her own moods and emotions.

Art and emotions

We have many words to describe different emotions, but very young children or people who have been abused or traumatized in some way often find it hard to say how they really feel. Discover how therapists (people who help others deal with their emotions) use art and drama to help people express their emotions in another way. Find out how artists such as Edvard Munch and Vincent van Gogh expressed emotions in their art. What would you paint to express anger, happiness, loneliness, or calm?

Quiz answers (see pages 56–57)

1) False: Emotions last seconds or minutes, but moods can last days.

2) a

3) True

4) False: High levels of serotonin make people feel happier.

5) True

6) False: It is an infant's strong emotional bond with his or her main caregiver that ensures the infant is well cared for.

7) a

8) b

9) False: They spend around 4.5 hours per day on screen time and four hours per week exercising.

10) c

11) True

12) b

13) b

14) True

index

11 September 2001 attacks 12, 29

abuse 13, 26, 27, 29, 36, 59

adrenaline 9, 40

aggression 23, 28, 37

alligators 9

Alzheimer's disease 51

amygdala 8, 31, 32, 36, 53

anger 5, 8, 9, 11, 12, 13, 21, 33, 37, 52

antidepressants 46, 47

anxiety 8, 12, 17, 19, 20, 22, 27, 29, 41, 42, 43, 45, 47, 50, 52, 59

attachment 16, 17, 18, 20, 30

autism 12

body image 28, 34, 35, 46, 48, 49

bonding 16, 17, 18, 20, 30, 32, 43, 55

"bucket lists" 44

bullying 25, 26, 27, 28, 39, 41

calmness 6, 10, 15, 38

cerebral cortex 10

complex phobias 7

confidence 18, 25, 26, 27, 39, 46, 50, 59

crime 18, 19, 41

cultures 13, 28, 29

cutting see self-harming

deaths 5, 42, 44, 55

dementia 51, 52, 53, 59

depression 4, 8, 19, 27, 29, 36, 37, 38, 39, 43, 46, 47, 58, 59

diet 12, 30, 47, 48, 58

disgust 11

distress 14, 17

education see school

empathy 5, 7, 24, 42

endorphins 23, 40

exercise 12, 23, 35, 46, 47

experience 5, 6, 11, 16, 17, 18, 22, 31, 52, 54, 55 see also memories

facial expressions 4, 6, 7, 10, 11, 12, 13, 14, 16, 20, 32

fear 6, 7, 10, 11, 17, 20, 26, 27, 32, 41, 48

"fight-or-flight" responses 10, 11, 34

frustration 20, 21, 34, 43, 44, 45, 48, 49

gangs 41

glands 9

gonadotropin 46

grief 7, 55

guilt 12, 25, 39, 41, 43

hand-holding 13

hippocampus 31, 36, 37, 51, 53

hormones 9, 10, 31, 32, 35, 36, 37, 43, 45, 46, 49

hypothalamus 8, 9, 26, 31

independence 14, 20, 30, 42, 48, 55

Jamaica study 19

jealousy 22

life expectancy 32, 48

meditation 13

memories 5, 31, 35, 36, 51, 52, 53 see also experience

menopause 45, 46, 49

midlife crises 44, 45, 47

money 42, 44, 45, 50, 58

mood 4, 26, 36, 37, 40, 42, 43, 47, 50, 51

multitasking 31

neurons 8, 9, 14, 31, 40, 46, 51, 53

neurotransmitters 8, 9, 10, 35, 36, 46, 47

noises see sounds

nursing homes 51, 53

omega-3 fatty acids 47

parenthood 43

peer pressure 41

phobias 7

physical appearance see body image

pituitary gland 9, 31

play 6, 15, 16, 19, 23

positive reinforcement 19

postnatal depression 43

poverty 28, 58

prefrontal cortex 31, 32, 33, 36

pregnancy 15, 40, 43

premenstrual syndrome (PMS) 37

puberty 30, 31, 32, 34, 37

racism 28, 29

range of emotions 5, 10, 20, 22

refugees 28, 29

relaxation 10, 14

"rest-and-digest" responses 10

risky activities 40, 41, 44

routines 17, 22, 50

sadness 5, 6, 11, 12, 15, 20, 34, 36, 45, 46, 48

schizophrenia 59

school 18, 19, 22, 23, 24, 25, 27, 29, 35, 36, 42

self-awareness 24, 30, 32, 37

self-esteem 19, 20, 27, 36, 45, 46

self-harming 36, 38–39, 59

self-regulation 25, 37

separation anxiety 17, 20

serotonin 9, 37, 46, 47

sexuality 13, 31, 32, 35, 36, 40, 41, 45, 46

sleep patterns 12, 17, 35

smiling 6, 10, 11, 13, 14, 16, 20

sounds 6, 11, 12, 13, 14, 15, 17, 20

strangers 17, 20, 51

stress 14, 17, 23, 30, 34, 35, 36, 37, 40, 43, 44, 47, 53, 54, 58, 59

strokes 51

substance abuse 28, 38, 40, 59

survival instincts 9, 10

synapses 8, 46

temperament 26, 48

temper tantrums 20, 21, 25

triggers 6, 7, 36

words 4, 11, 17, 21, 27